THOMA

Quilting
R·H·Y·T·H·M

98 Innovative Designs
for Free-Motion & Digital
Stitching

stashBOOKS®

an imprint of C&T Publishing

Text and artwork copyright © 2023 by Thomas Knauer

Photography © 2023 by C&T Publishing, Inc.

Publisher: Amy Barrett-Daffin

Creative Director: Gailen Runge

Senior Editor: Roxane Cerda

Associate Editor: Karly Wallace

Cover/Book Designer: April Mostek

Production Coordinator: Zinnia Heinzmann

Illustrator: Thomas Knauer and Kirstie Pettersen

Photography Coordinator: Lauren Herberg

Photography Assistant: Rachel Ackley

Front cover photography by Lauren Herberg

Photography by Lauren Herberg of C&T Publishing, Inc., unless otherwise noted

Published by Stash Books, an imprint of C&T Publishing, Inc., P.O. Box 1456, Lafayette, CA 94549

Library of Congress Cataloging-in-Publication Data

Names: Knauer, Thomas, author.
Title: Quilting rhythm : 98 innovative designs for free-motion & digital stitching / Thomas Knauer.
Description: Lafayette, CA : Stash Books, [2023] | Summary: "Featured inside are 98 innovative and fresh quilting designs that provide a vast array of texture and rhythm to the quilt top as they range from geometric to graphically-inspired. These designs are equally appealing to both free-motion quilters and quilters who prefer computerized quilting"-- Provided by publisher.
Identifiers: LCCN 2022031336 | ISBN 9781644033821 (trade paperback) | ISBN 9781644033838 (ebook)
Subjects: LCSH: Machine quilting--Patterns. | Quilting--Design.
Classification: LCC TT835 .K5637 2023 | DDC 746.46/041--dc23/eng/20220803
LC record available at https://lccn.loc.gov/2022031336

Printed in China

10 9 8 7 6 5 4 3 2 1

Epigraph

Design creates culture. Culture shapes values. Values determine the future. -Robert L. Peters

Dedication

For Sol LeWitt. You taught me that careful input will inevitably lead to exceptional output.

Acknowledgements

First and foremost, I need to thank my editor, Roxane, for going to bat for my first book with C&T. Her doing so gave me the opportunity to procrastinate writing it by working on this second book. Your advice and support have been invaluable along the winding route to bringing this book to fruition.

Once more I have to thank April Mostek for her design sensitivity in putting this book together. You are an absolute pleasure to work with. And of course great thanks to everyone at C&T who had a hand in making this unexpected book happen.

A further thanks to Jen Strauser for stitching out a bunch of the designs in *Quilting Rhythm* and in *Quilt Out Loud*, assuring me that they did indeed work. You are a rock star.

An incalculable thank you to my beloved wife who spent so much time helping me sort, scrutinize, and ultimately select the designs that made it into this book. You were essential in transforming a tsunami of designs into a tide pool.

I also want to thank the Art Department at Kenyon College for helping me to develop the skills needed to put together an artistic practice that could weather the decades, change when needed, and always have a voice.

Finally, thanks to my children for just being flat out awesome. I love you more than there are stitches in my quilts.

Contents

LINES

SQUARES AND RECTANGLES

DIAMONDS AND TRIANGLES

SCRIBBLES

Design Gallery

LINES

Design 01
33

Design 02
34

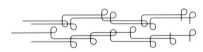

Design 03
35

Design 04
36

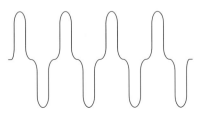

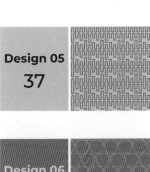

Design 05
37

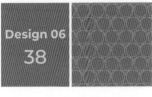

Design 06
38

Design 07
39

Design 08
40

Design 09
41

Design 10
42

Design 11
43

Design 12
44

Design 13
45

Design 14
46

Design 15
47

Design 16
48

Design 17
49

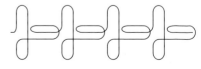

Design 18
50

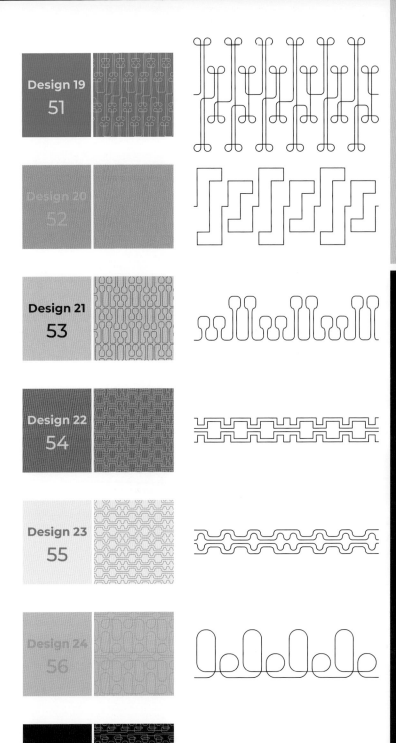

Design 19
51

Design 20
52

Design 21
53

Design 22
54

Design 23
55

Design 24
56

Design 25
57

 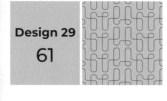
QUILTING RHYTHM

SQUARES AND RECTANGLES

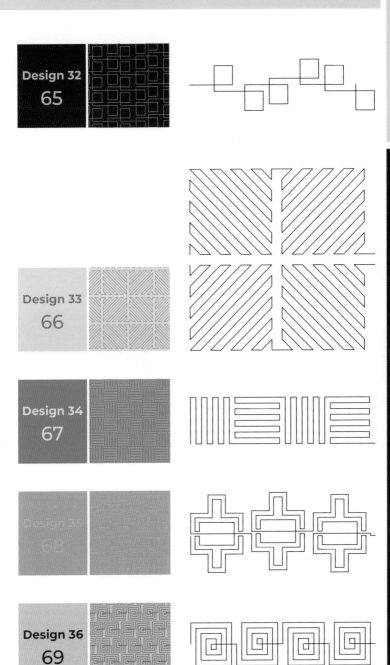

Design 32
65

Design 33
66

Design 34
67

Design 35
68

Design 36
69

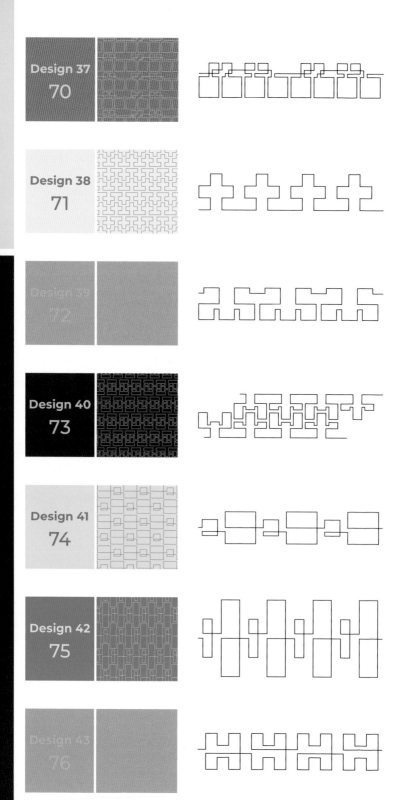

Design 37
70

Design 38
71

Design 39
72

Design 40
73

Design 41
74

Design 42
75

Design 43
76

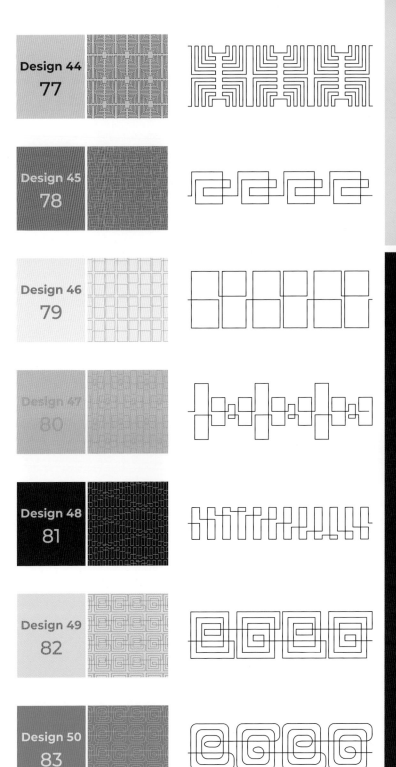

Design 44
77

Design 45
78

Design 46
79

Design 47
80

Design 48
81

Design 49
82

Design 50
83

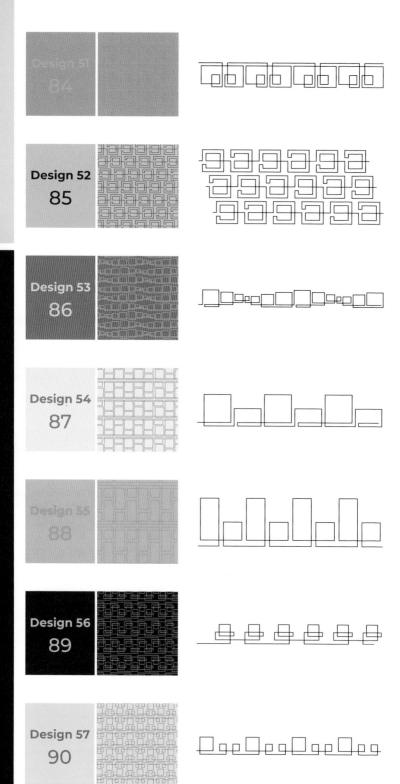

Design 51
84

Design 52
85

Design 53
86

Design 54
87

Design 55
88

Design 56
89

Design 57
90

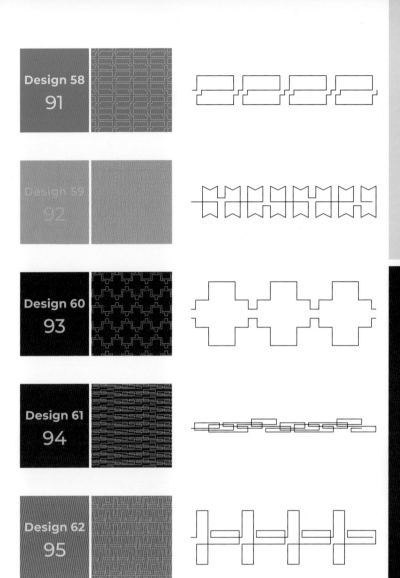

Design 58
91

Design 59
92

Design 60
93

Design 61
94

Design 62
95

DIAMONDS AND TRIANGLES

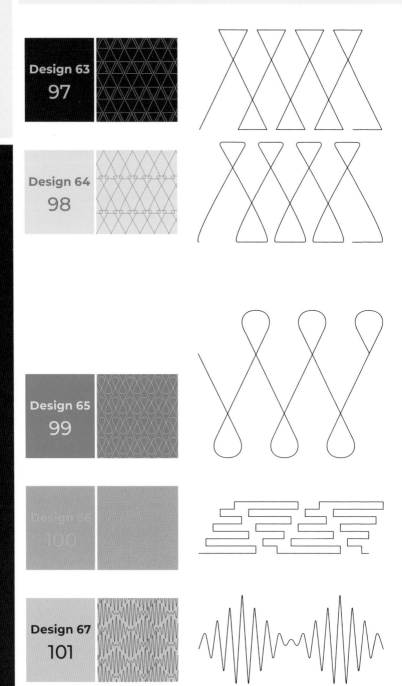

Design 63
97

Design 64
98

Design 65
99

Design 66
100

Design 67
101

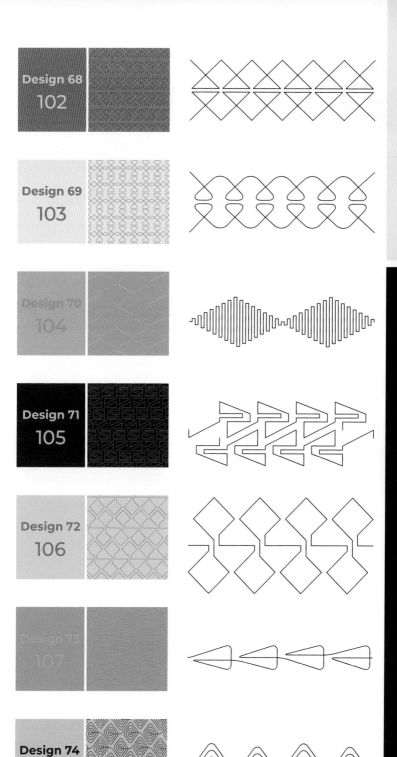

Design 68
102

Design 69
103

Design 70
104

Design 71
105

Design 72
106

Design 73
107

Design 74
108

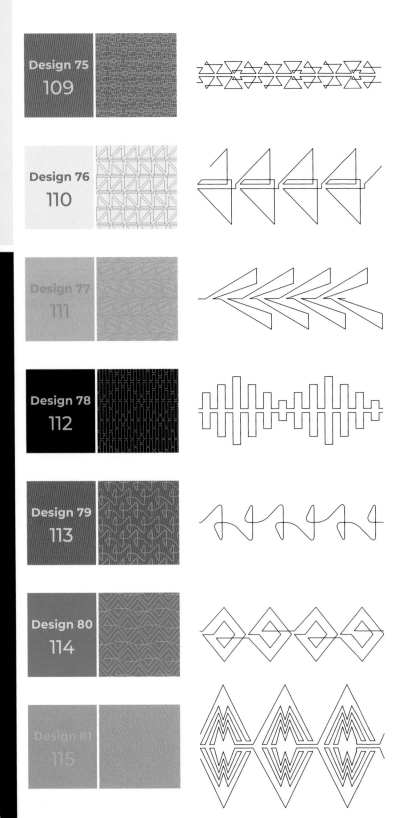

Design 75
109

Design 76
110

Design 77
111

Design 78
112

Design 79
113

Design 80
114

Design 81
115

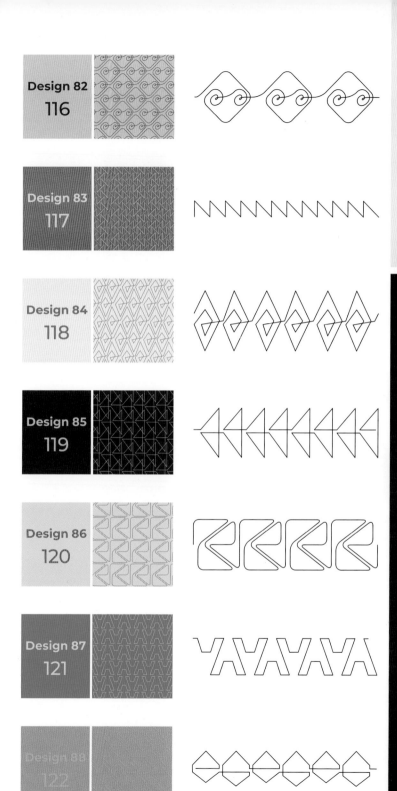

Design 82
116

Design 83
117

Design 84
118

Design 85
119

Design 86
120

Design 87
121

Design 88
122

SCRIBBLES

Design 89
124

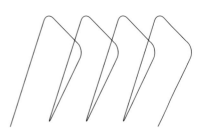

Design 90
125

Design 91
126

Design 92
127

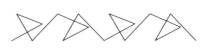

Design 93
128

Design 94
129

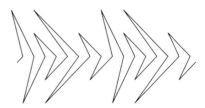

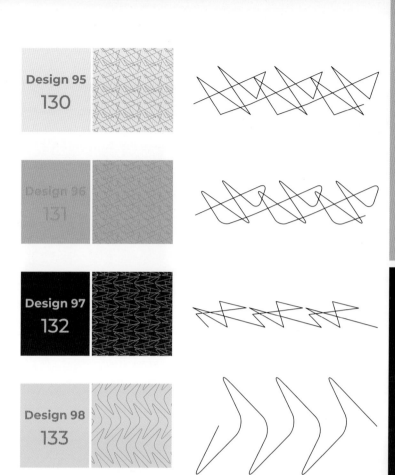

Design 95
130

Design 96
131

Design 97
132

Design 98
133

Introduction

Since I began quilting around a decade ago, I have been drawn most consistently to allover quilting. From the simplest straight lines to designs of extraordinary complexity, I love the way allover quilting provides a cohesive thread that runs throughout the patchwork or appliqué. The quilt top is treated as a unified whole rather than an accumulation of parts.

While I admire quilts in which each square, triangle, and every other conceivable shape is quilted individually, I also find that they feel somewhat fragmentary. These specific quilts utilize motifs for different areas. Following the piecing, the parts are separated from each other, making a beautiful quilt disconnected. Alternatively, allover quilting searches for a line or pattern that speaks beautifully with all parts of a quilt.

Allover quilting goes hand in hand with modern quilting. The minimal patchwork of modern quilts shares the same goal as these motifs, to make the unity of design a focal point. A single motif, line, or pattern gives the subtleties of the piecing space to breathe, receiving texture and rhythm from the quilting without adding visual disruption. These designs will not overwhelm your quilt, but will instead create an interplay of stitching and fabric that yields a harmonious whole.

This technique is particularly important in my quilts, in which there is very little patchwork and which often consist of text appliquéd to a single-color background. As such, many of my quilts give no indication of just how the top should be quilted. Over the years, I have designed hundreds of quilting motifs. Each motif gets its own custom treatment in the hope of finding just the right line to run through the quilt and render it complete.

In *Quilting Rhythm*, I share 98 of my favorite abstract designs along with each motif's vector artwork, all downloadable from the C&T site; for information about downloading the designs, see Accessing the Digital Designs (page 29). The motifs in this collection range from geometric to graphically inspired. This design library is designed for both free-motion and computerized quilters. Whether you are a free-motion quilter or a computerized quilter, the designs are easy to use. For computerized quilting, the vector artwork is easily convertible to any file format. The paper designs are ready for experienced hand-guided quilters to follow.

P·A·R·T O·N·E

What to Know Before You Stitch

Advice for Free-Motion Quilters

The key to mastering any motif is practice, practice, practice. While many of the designs in this book lean toward geometric complexity, they are all achievable. I suggest you start by tracing your chosen design; grab a pencil and some tracing paper, and familiarize your hand with the movement of the design. From there, jump to drawing the design until you are comfortable repeating it with a fair degree of accuracy. Finally, spend some time practicing on muslin; there is nothing like stitching it out for learning a new motif. It may take some time and practice, but I hope your effort will be consistently rewarded with beautifully stitched quilts.

Beyond that, I recommend playing to your strengths. If geometric designs are your forte, there are plenty of designs that should speak to you. If you prefer flowing designs and curves, there are designs for you as well. The goal of this book is to present motifs that will stretch boundaries while presenting a broad palette of new designs that go beyond the ordinary.

Advice for Computerized Quilters

No feathers or florals, these designs are unique and perfect for edge-to-edge quilting. Made with computerized quilters in mind, *Quilting Rhythm* is beyond your typical quilting motif book. Inside, quilters have access to digital design files that are ready to be converted to stitches. These motifs add a wide array of possibilities to your computerized quilting practice.

Motifs in the book are entirely scalable to fit your needs by becoming denser or looser, more or less intricate, to perfectly complement each of the quilts you stitch. Browse through the motifs and find your favorite, then get the files, and put them right to work on your computerized machine.

For those who work with computer-guided machines, you can download the vector artwork for the motifs and hit the ground running.

How-to: Digitized Designs

Digitizing software converts vector artwork to stitches and is rather straightforward. With the software I use—Art and Stitch, which ships with many computerized machines—I follow the steps below. Your software may be different, but the basic steps should be similar to those below.

1 I begin by importing the artwork into the digitizing environment.

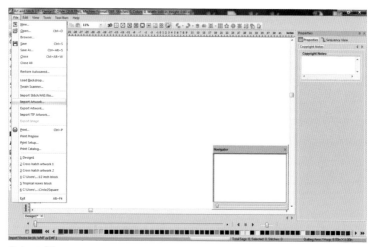

Select file

Import vector artwork

2 Next, I select the artwork I want to convert and hit the *Convert to Stitches* button. *Note: If you have different software, select the option that will convert your artwork to stitches.*

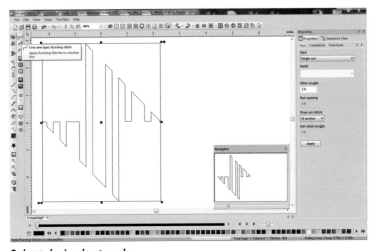

Select desired artwork

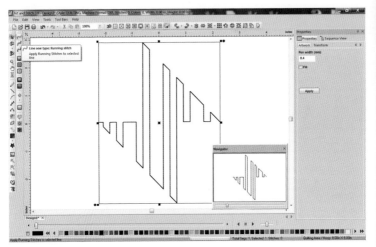

Click the *Convert to Stitches* button

3 Once the artwork is converted to stitches, save the file as the file type that is compatible with your machine. Note that I have saved my file as a HQF, which works with Handi Quilter machines.

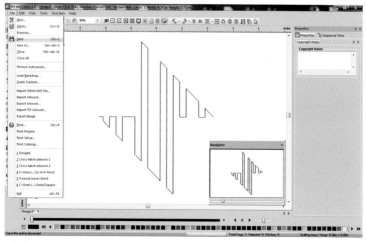

Click *Save As*

Select the file type that is compatible with your machine

4 Finished!

If you work with a computer-guided machine, you can download the vector artwork for the motifs and hit the ground running.

How-to: Accessing the Digital Designs

The quilting designs in this book can be accessed through tiny URLs, located at the beginning of each chapter of quilting designs, Lines (page 32), Squares and Rectangles (page 64), Diamonds and Triangles (page 96), and Scribbles (page 123).

To access the digital files through the tiny URL, just type the tiny URL (a web address) into your browser window. When you click *enter* the SVG files for that chapter will download to your device. Open the zip file and you can select just the design you want from the book.

The digital quilting designs in this book may be used to make items for personal use only and may not be used for the purpose of personal profit. Items created to benefit nonprofit groups, or that will be publicly displayed, must be conspicuously labeled with the following credit: "Quilting Designs copyright © 2023 by Thomas Knauer from the book *Quilting Rhythm* from C&T Publishing, Inc." Permission for all other purposes must be requested in writing from C&T Publishing, Inc.

Attention Professional Quilters: Please note the following exception—publisher and author give permission to use the digital files from this book when provided by the customer to be used exclusively for that customer's quilt.

Final Thoughts

Each chapter offers a different approach to stitching wonderfully textural quilting. Some of the designs are based on structure, while others emphasize movement and energy. This unique group of designs features options that range from tightly angular to loosely curvilinear. A goal of these designs is to expand your quilting vocabulary beyond the traditional flowers and feathers. *Quilting Rhythm* is about giving quilters a fresh perspective on allover quilting that blends modern design principles with a practical quilter's concerns.

P·A·R·T T·W·O

Quilting Designs

Lines

These texture-based designs emphasize the careful use of white space to guarantee your quilts do not get too stiff, however dense you choose to quilt them. In this collection, the lines make their way across quilts, ambling from one side to the other and at times turning back upon themselves in loops and swirls. Line designs create a sense of perpetual movement, not just in one direction or the other but all over any given quilt.

DIGITAL FILES—LINES
To access the digital files through the tiny URL, just type the tiny URL (a web address) into your browser window. When you click *enter* the SVG files for this chapter will download to your device. Open the zip file and you can select just the design you want from the book. • tinyurl.com/11551-pattern1-download

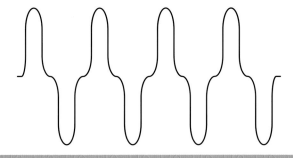

QUILTING RHYTHM

05

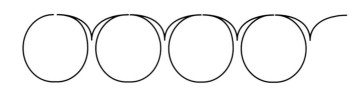

06

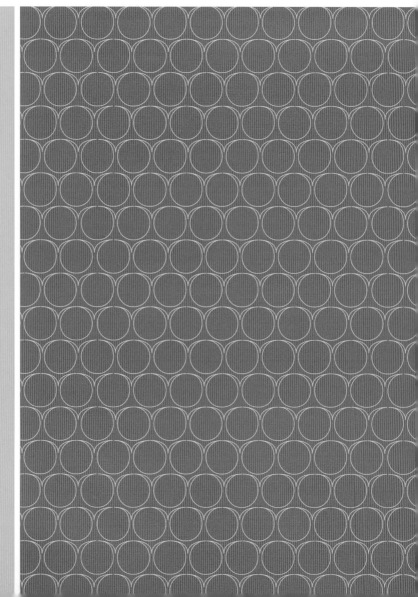

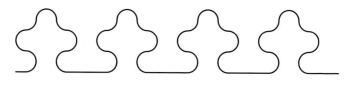

QUILTING RHYTHM

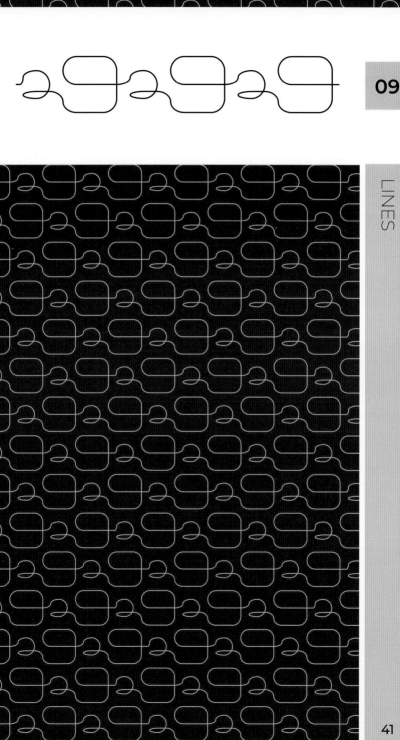

LINES

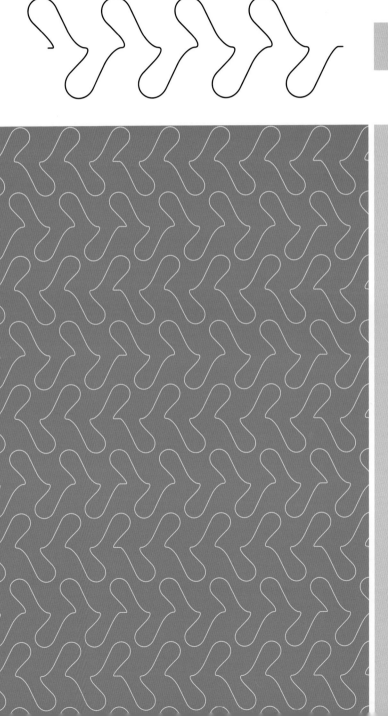

LINES

12

QUILTING RHYTHM

QUILTING RHYTHM

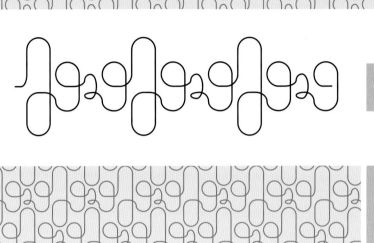

15

16

QUILTING RHYTHM

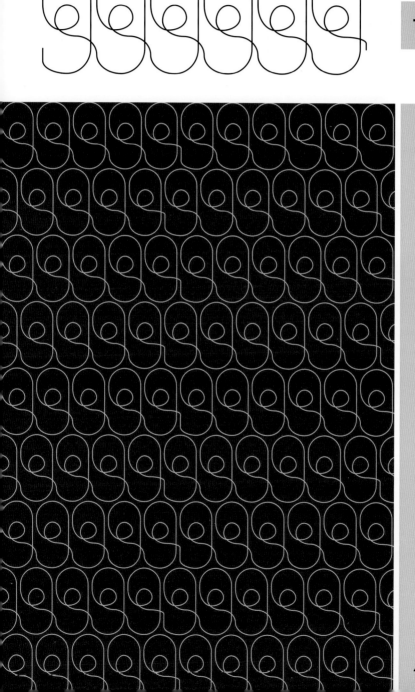

LINES

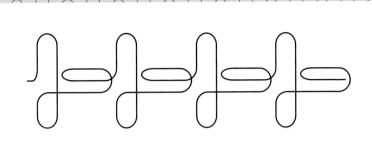

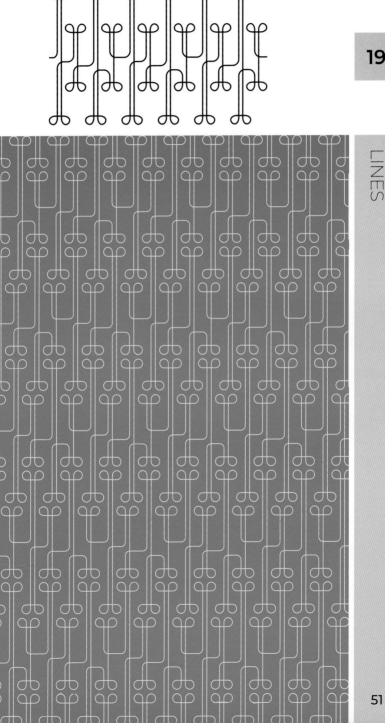

LINES

20

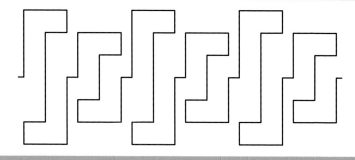

QUILTING RHYTHM

LINES

22

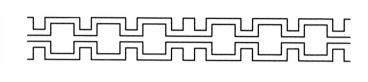

QUILTING RHYTHM

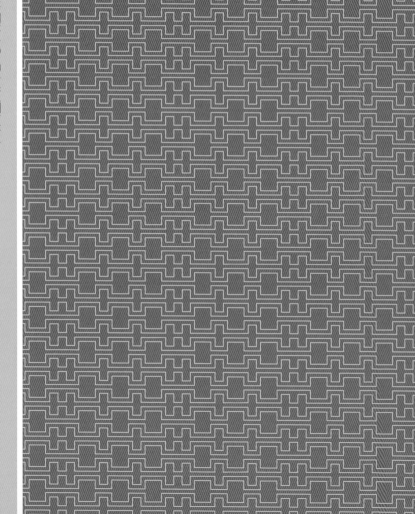

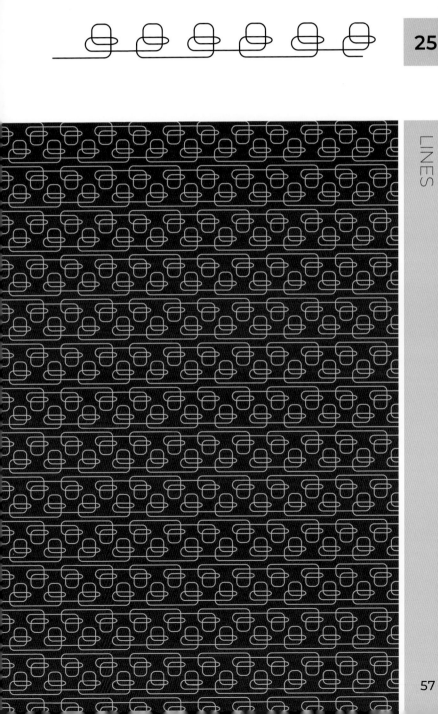

25

26

LINES

28

30

LINES

Squares and Rectangles

The motifs in this chapter move over your quilt and also create an aesthetically stable structure. The squares and rectangles that are featured stack and build upon each other, creating larger designs through the relationships between the elements. Pair these with understated designs for a formal order or use them in contrast to the wildest quilt tops.

DIGITAL FILES—SQUARES AND RECTANGLES
To access the digital files through the tiny URL, just type the tiny URL (a web address) into your browser window. When you click *enter* the SVG files for this chapter will download to your device. Open the zip file and you can select just the design you want from the book. • tinyurl.com/11551-pattern2-download

SQUARES AND RECTANGLES

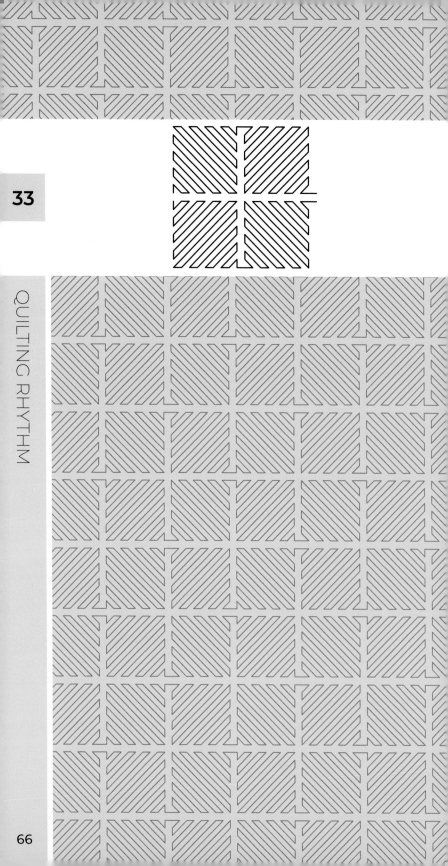

QUILTING RHYTHM

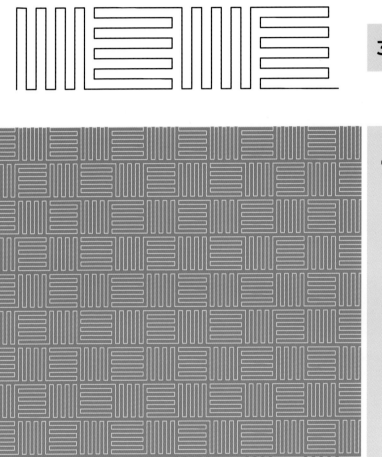

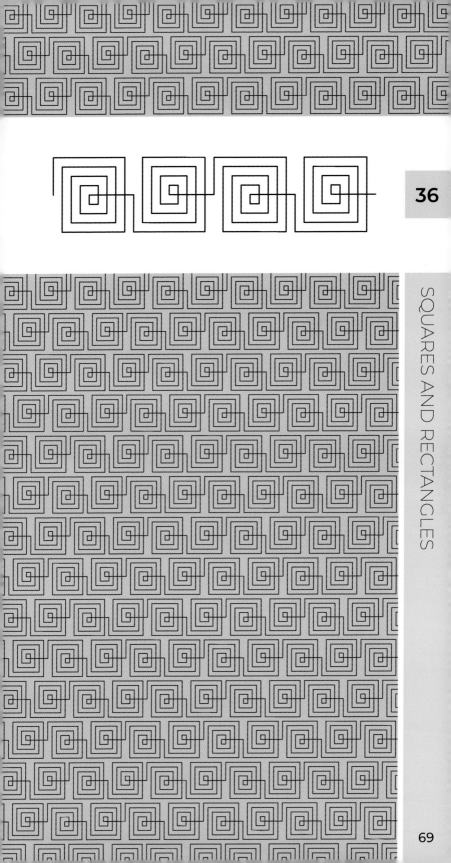

36

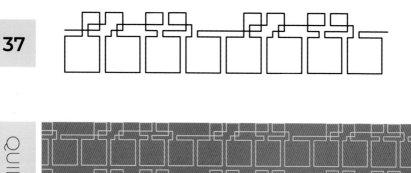

37

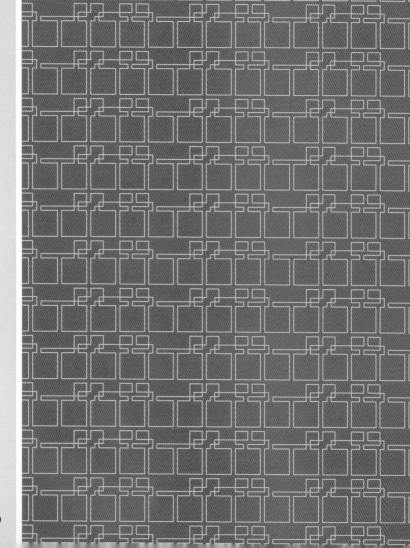

SQUARES AND RECTANGLES

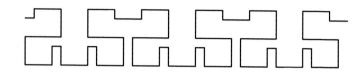

QUILTING RHYTHM

SQUARES AND RECTANGLES

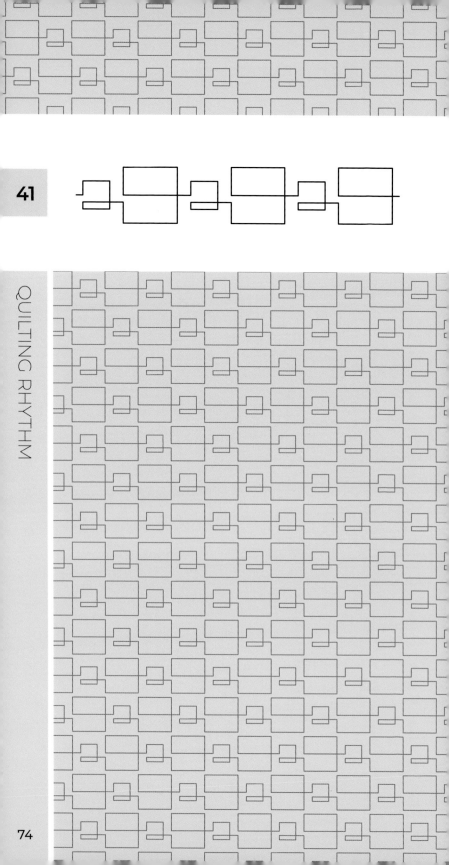

QUILTING RHYTHM

42

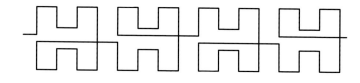

QUILTING RHYTHM

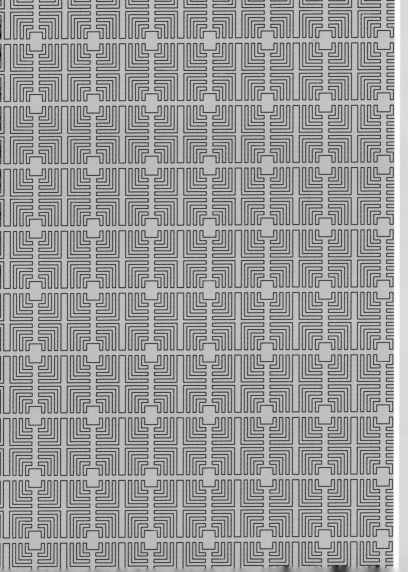

SQUARES AND RECTANGLES

45

QUILTING RHYTHM

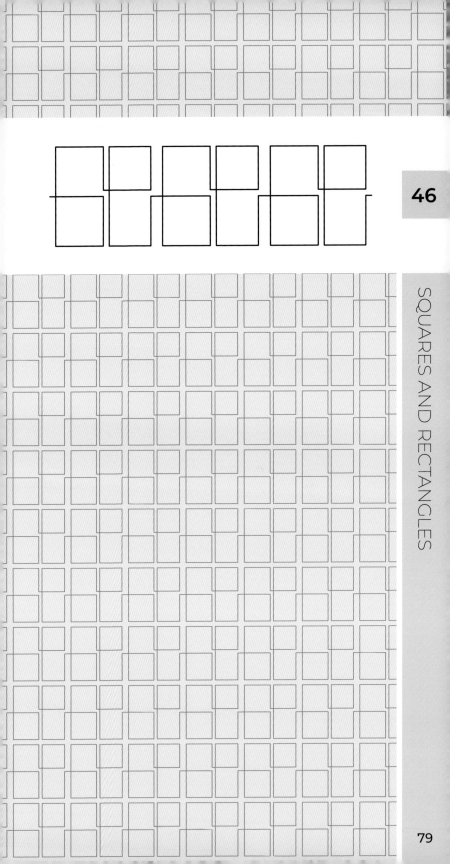

SQUARES AND RECTANGLES

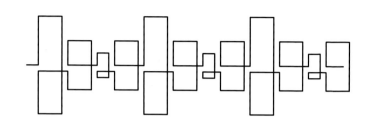

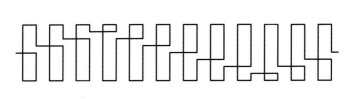

SQUARES AND RECTANGLES

49

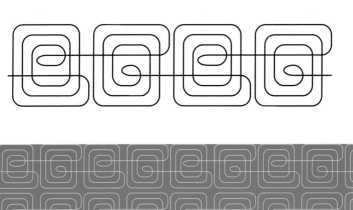

SQUARES AND RECTANGLES

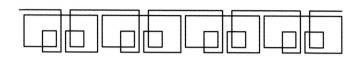

SQUARES AND RECTANGLES

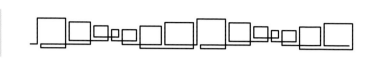

QUILTING RHYTHM

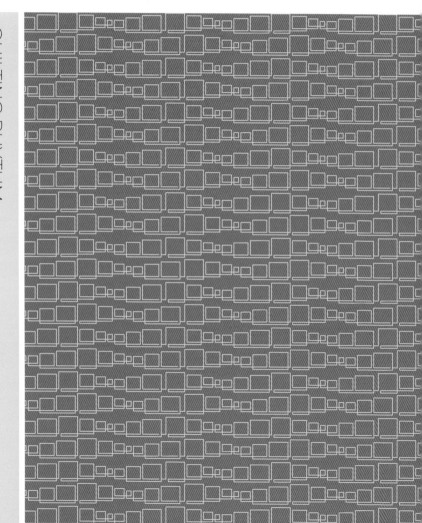

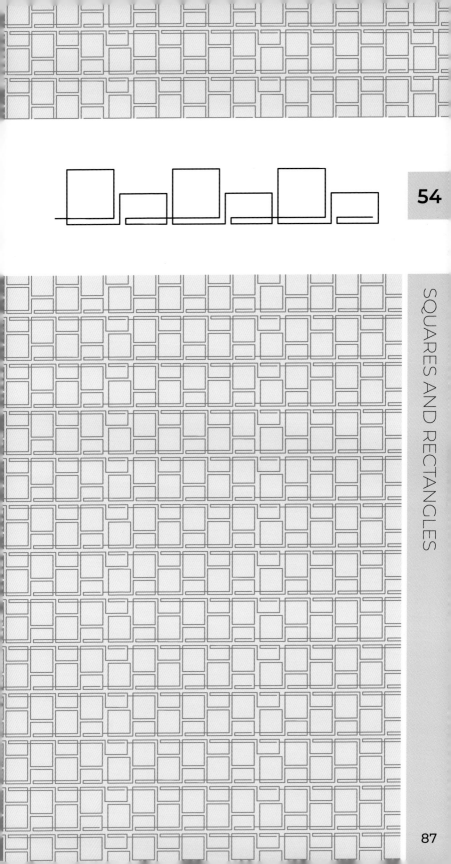

54

QUILTING RHYTHM

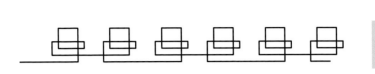

56

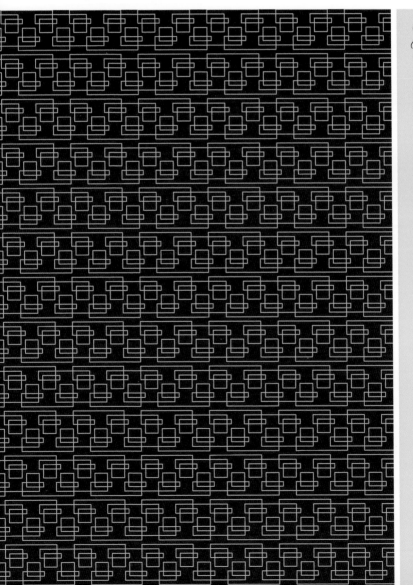

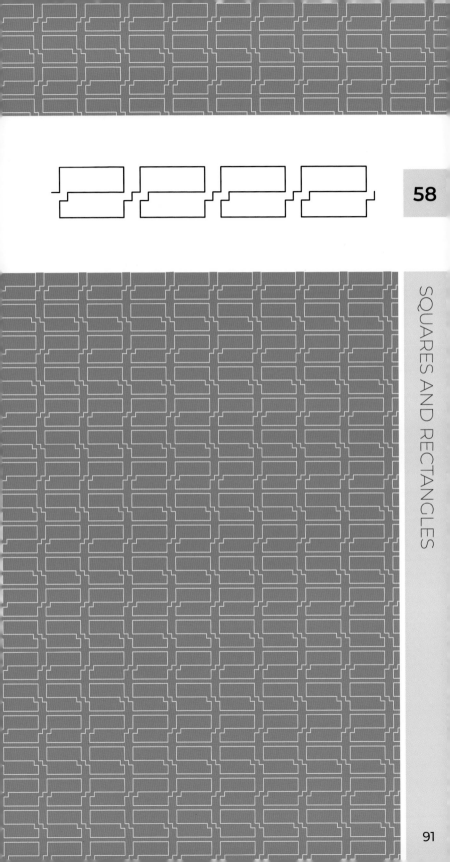

58

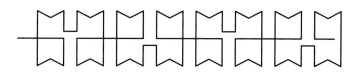

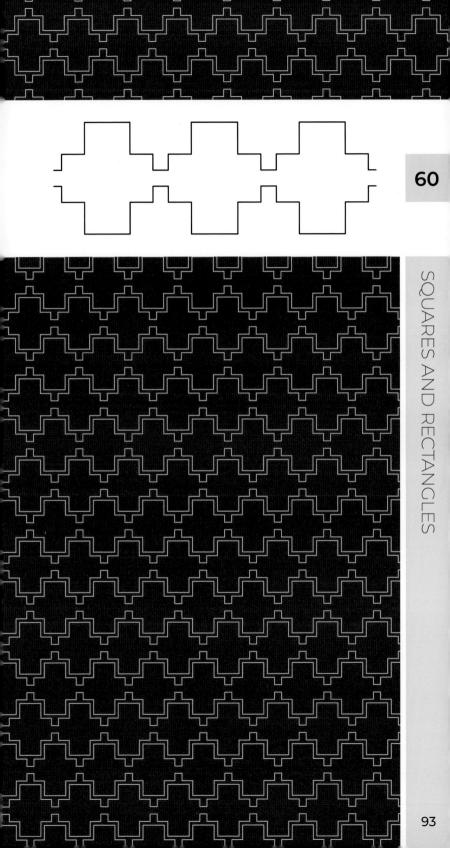

SQUARES AND RECTANGLES

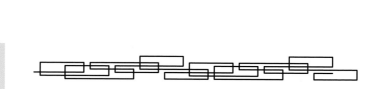

61

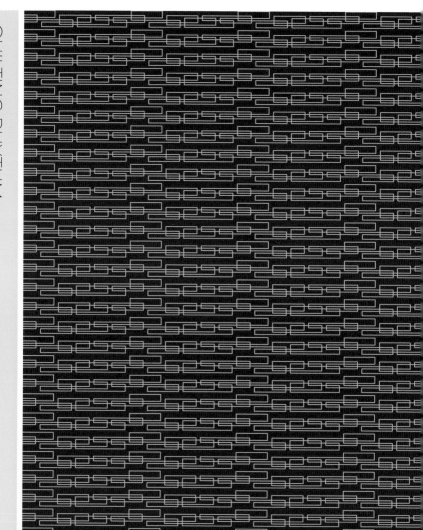

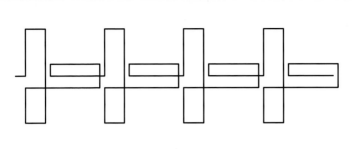

SQUARES AND RECTANGLES

Diamonds and Triangles

With an abundance of diagonals, these designs defy constraint and impart a palpable energy to your quilts. The majority of quilt tops follow a horizontal/vertical orientation; these motifs, however, offer perfect counters with a variety of angles and shapes, stitching one rhythm onto that of the piecing.

DIGITAL FILES—DIAMONDS AND TRIANGLES

To access the digital files through the tiny URL, just type the tiny URL (a web address) into your browser window. When you click *enter* the SVG files for this chapter will download to your device. Open the zip file and you can select just the design you want from the book. • tinyurl.com/11551-pattern3-download

DIAMONDS AND TRIANGLES

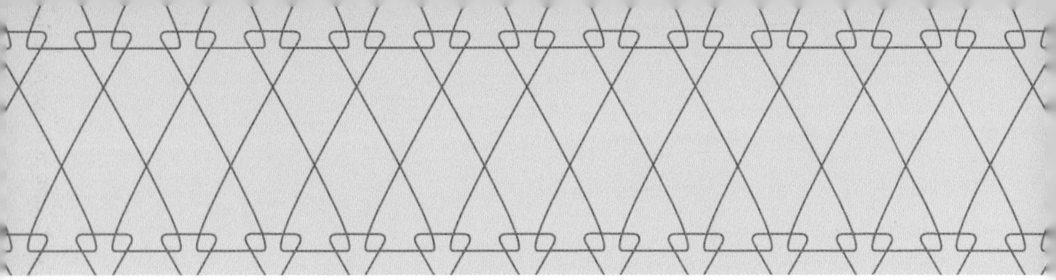

64

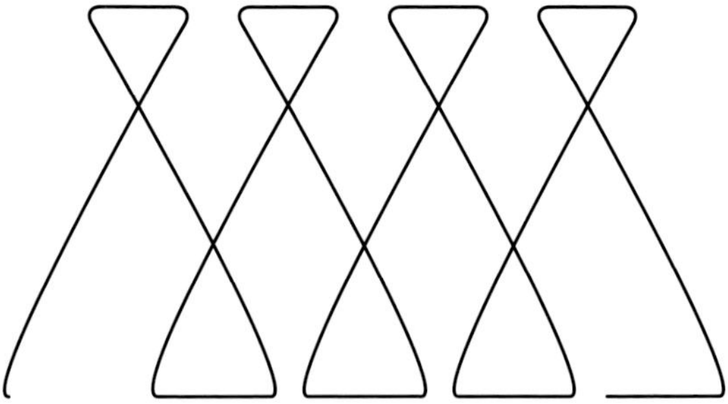

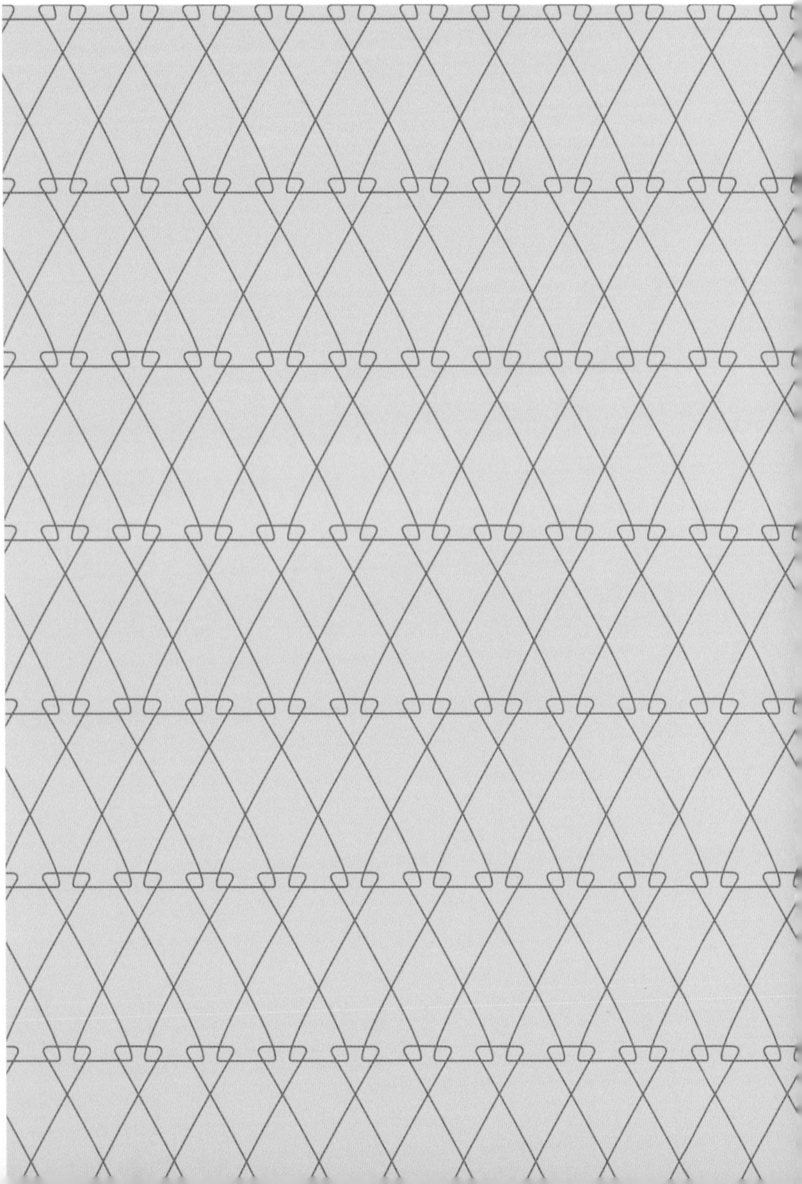

DIAMONDS AND TRIANGLES

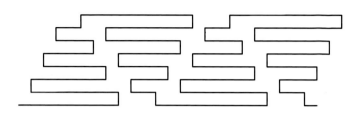

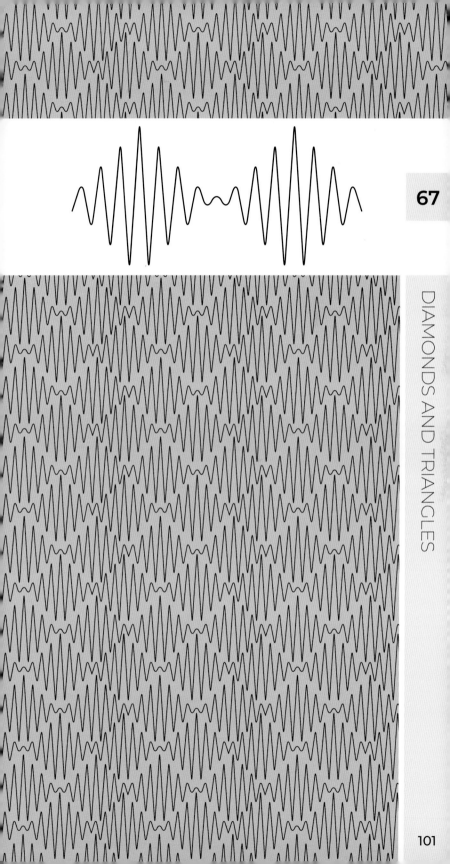

DIAMONDS AND TRIANGLES

QUILTING RHYTHM

DIAMONDS AND TRIANGLES

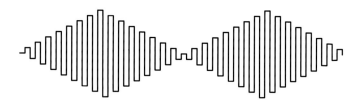

70

QUILTING RHYTHM

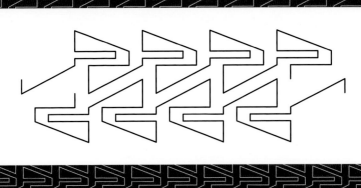

DIAMONDS AND TRIANGLES

QUILTING RHYTHM

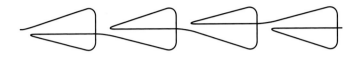

QUILTING RHYTHM

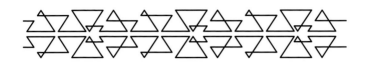

DIAMONDS AND TRIANGLES

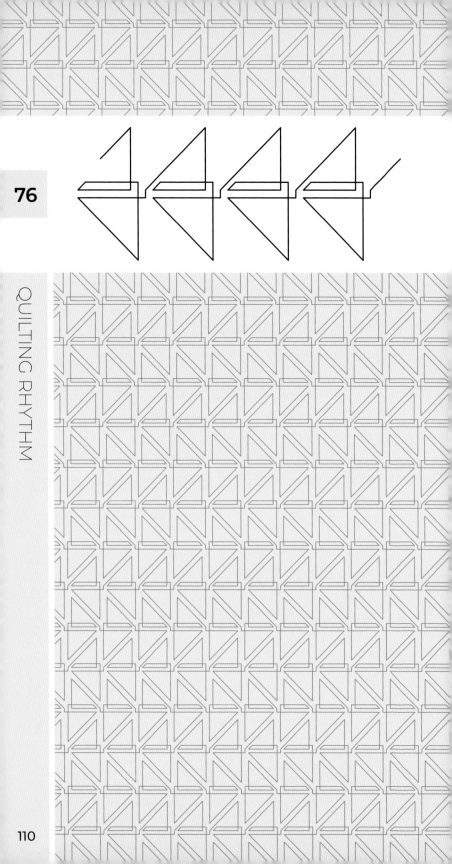

QUILTING RHYTHM

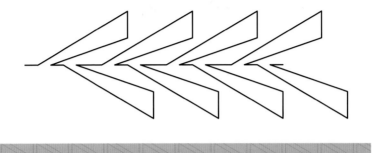

DIAMONDS AND TRIANGLES

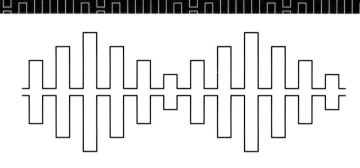

QUILTING RHYTHM

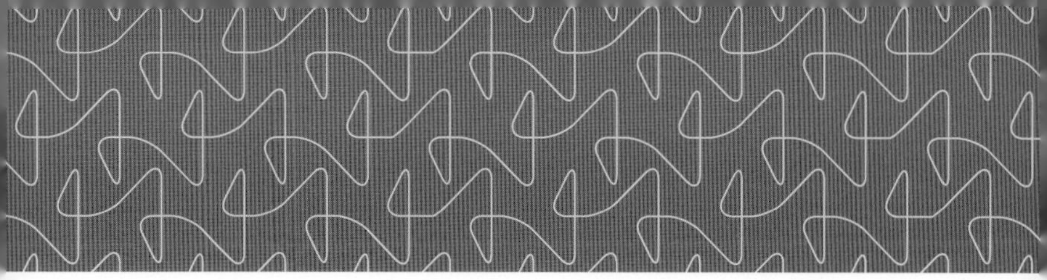

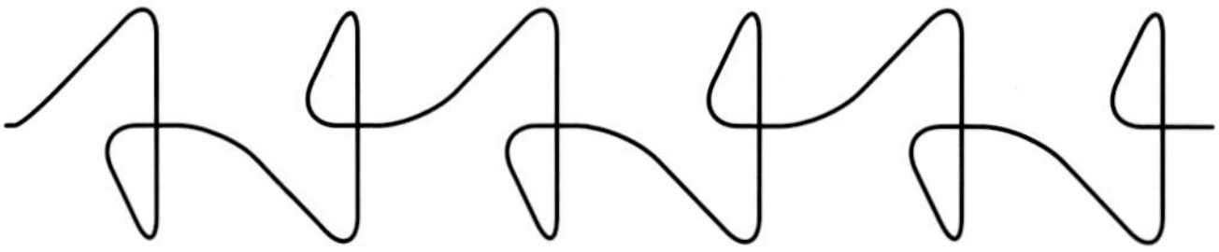

79

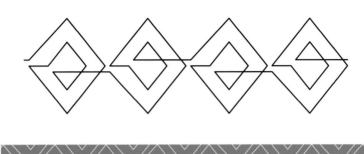

QUILTING RHYTHM

DIAMONDS AND TRIANGLES

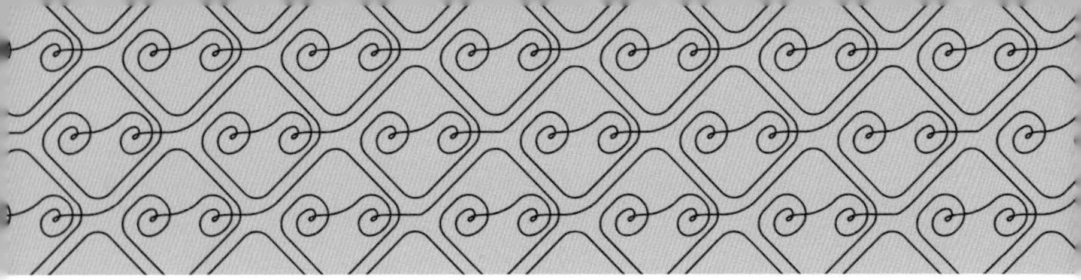

82

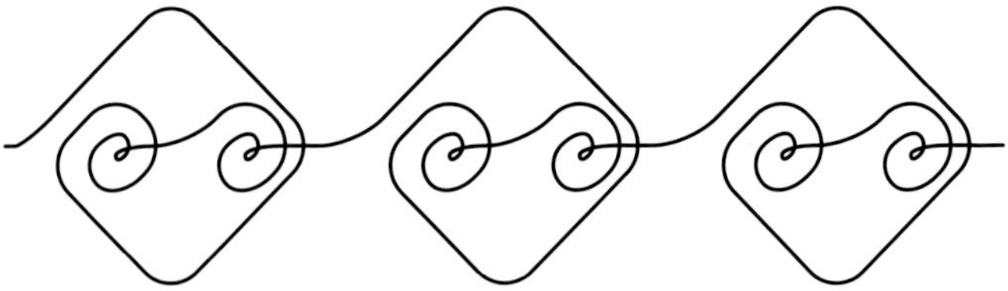

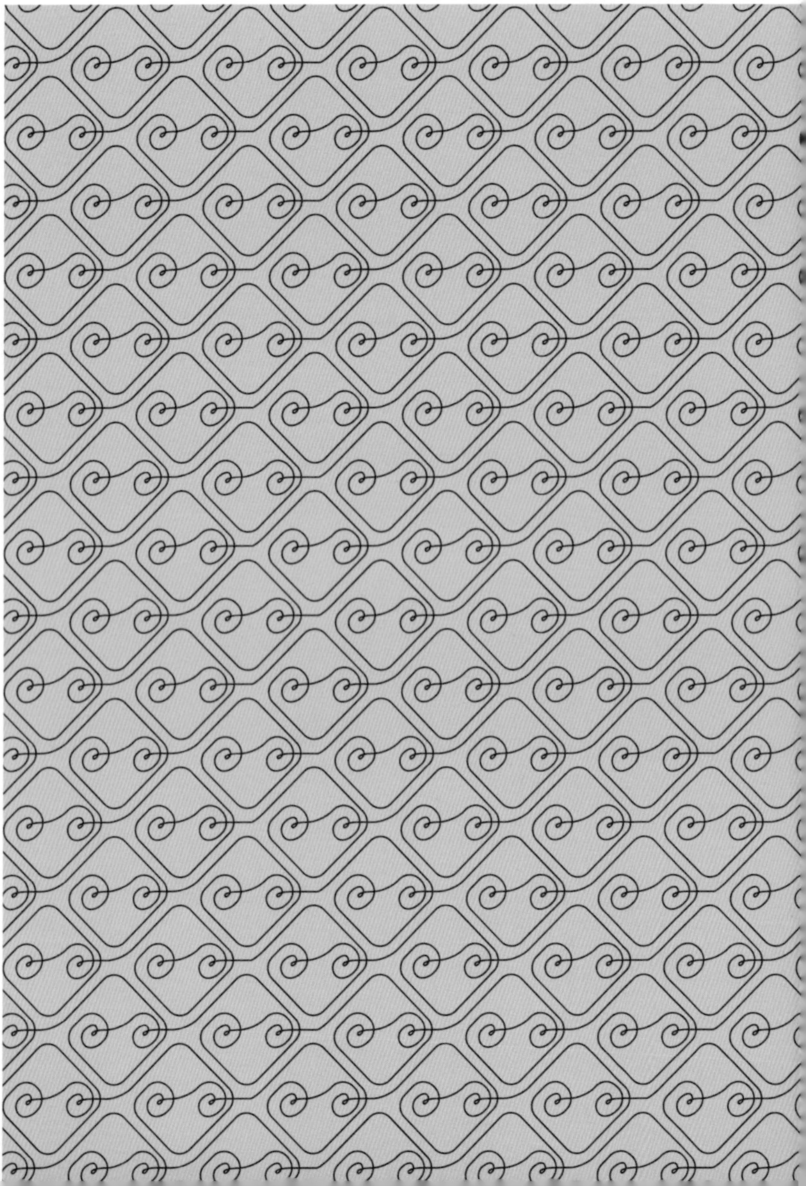

DIAMONDS AND TRIANGLES

84

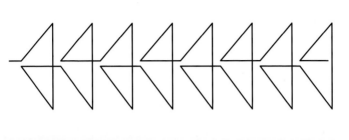

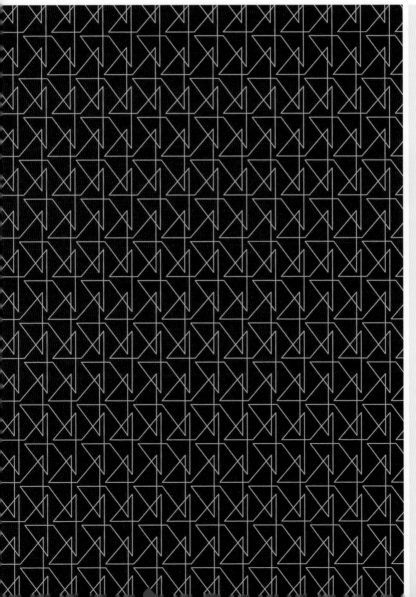

DIAMONDS AND TRIANGLES

DIAMONDS AND TRIANGLES

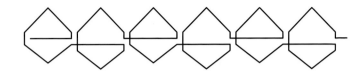

88

QUILTING RHYTHM

Scribbles

Full of energy and movement, the scribble designs are my favorite. They verge on chaos while still holding onto a minimal degree of structure. In this chapter, you will find unique textures with shapes and subdivisions that are entirely unexpected. While a scribble motif is not the best choice for every quilt, when it is strategically deployed, the design can truly activate the right quilt.

DIGITAL FILES—SCRIBBLES
To access the digital files through the tiny URL, just type the tiny URL (a web address) into your browser window. When you click *enter* the SVG files for this chapter will download to your device. Open the zip file and you can select just the design you want from the book. • tinyurl.com/11551-pattern4-download

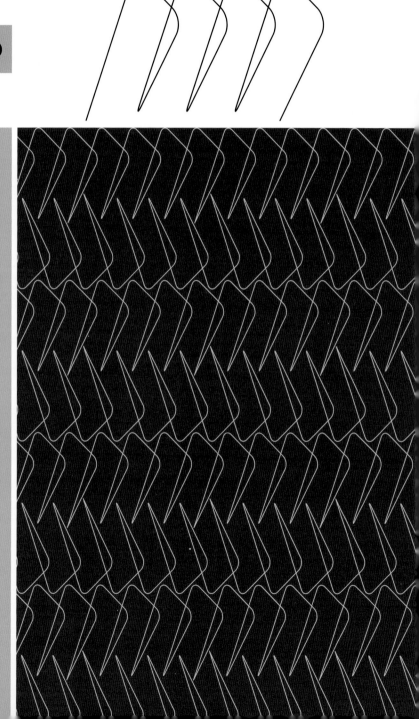

QUILTING RHYTHM

SCRIBBLES

QUILTING RHYTHM

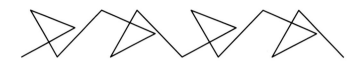

SCRIBBLES

QUILTING RHYTHM

SCRIBBLES

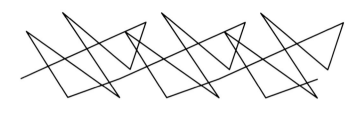

QUILTING RHYTHM

97

QUILTING RHYTHM

SCRIBBLES

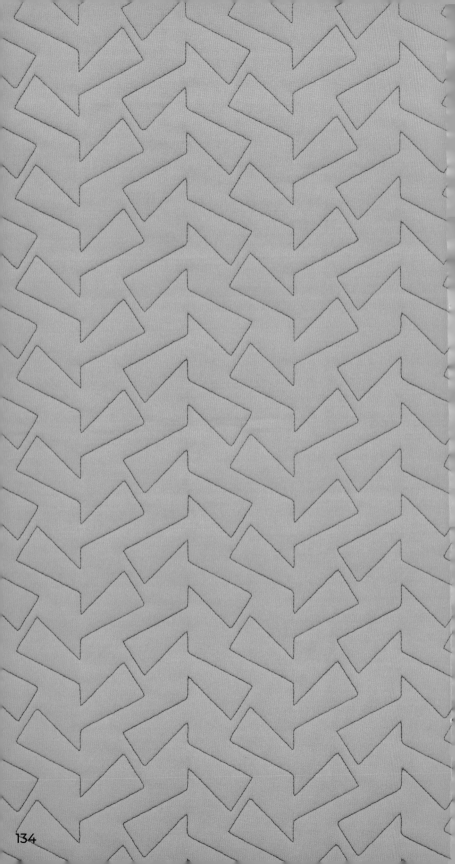

About the Author

Thomas Knauer lives in a small village in Upstate New York with his wife, two children, a rabbit, and a dragon. He spends much of his time exploring the minutiae of letters and numbers, words and sentences. He loves words in just about any form, from letterpress printing to multimedia development. So, it is no surprise that his work has

Photo by Katherine Terrell

taken a turn down the path of text-based quilts.

He began his professional life teaching design at Drake University before turning to quilting. He has designed fabrics for several leading manufacturers, and his work has been exhibited in quilt shows and museums across the country, including the International Quilt Museum, San Jose Museum of Quilts and Textiles, and the Quilt Festival in Houston.

His work typically focuses on issues of social justice and violence; his most recent body of work deals with the recent police shootings of unarmed African Americans. Knauer has authored several books prior to *Quilt Out Loud* and plans to keep writing as long as people will let him.

You can find him online at www.thomasknauersews.com.

CREATIVE SPARK

ONLINE LEARNING

Quilting courses to become an expert quilter...

From their studio to yours, Creative Spark instructors are teaching you how to create and become a master of your craft. So not only do you get a look inside their creative space, you also get to be a part of engaging courses that would typically be a one or multi-day workshop from the comfort of your home.

Creative Spark is not your one-size-fits-all online learning experience. We welcome you to be who you are, share, create, and belong.

Scan for a gift from us!

creativespark.ctpub.com